Non-fiction Voyage 1

Series Advisers:
Shirley Bickley and Raewyn Hickey

Contents

Non-chronological reports   Frances Ridley

Surprise Yourself!	2
Travel with a Twist	6

Instructions   Catherine Baker

Fizzy Stuff	10
Tip of the Tongue	12

Thesaurus texts   Huw Thomas

Spice Up Your Story: Lively Verbs	14
Spice Up Your Story: Expressive Adjectives	16

Letters   Elaine Canham

The Viking Sword	18
The Tudor Ring	21

Alphabetical texts   Huw Thomas

Magical Cards: People	24
Magical Cards: Mythical Creatures	28
Index	32

OXFORD UNIVERSITY PRESS

Surprise Yourself!

Imagine you have won a holiday in a competition.
You can choose one of three holidays.
Which one will you choose?

Fun in the snow in the French Alps

Wildlife and adventure on Vancouver Island

Learn to be a superhero in Yorkshire!

There are lots of things to think about:

- Who will be going on the holiday?
- What will the weather be like?
- Where will you be staying and what will it be like?
- What do you enjoy doing?

Family Fun in the Snow

On this holiday, the whole family can learn snow sports in the French Alps.

The most popular activities are:
- skiing
- snowboarding
- riding on a skidoo
- ice-skating.

The hotel has a swimming pool and a games room. Children's discos take place twice a week.

Tips!
- Be warned! You will fall over a lot when you are learning!
- Take a packed lunch on to the mountain – eating out is very expensive.
- Don't wear a scarf when you're skiing – it's dangerous.
- Wear sunscreen – you can burn even though it's cold.

Important information

Number of weeks	Accommodation	Weather conditions	Things you need
1	Hotel	Sunny but very cold and snowy	Ski clothing Sunglasses Sunscreen Lip protection

Vancouver Adventure

Vancouver Island, Canada, has mountains, rocky coastlines and beaches. There are also lots of interesting animals, birds and fish to see. This holiday on Vancouver Island includes:

- hiking in the mountains
- learning how to kayak in the sea
- whale-watching trips
- swimming in the hot springs
- boat tours to look for black bears.

If you're lucky, you may see killer whales, seals, sea lions and bald eagles.

You might even see a huge sun starfish. They can grow up to 24 arms!

Tips!

This is not a luxury holiday! You will have to:
- put up your own tent and take it down again
- help to cook and wash up
- help to clean the bus!

Important information

Number of weeks	Accommodation	Weather conditions	Things you need
2	Tent	Cool

Rain likely | Sleeping bag
Warm jacket
Waterproofs
Strong shoes
Rucksack |

Train to be a Superhero!

This is a holiday for children aged 8 to 12 at an adventure park in Whitby, Yorkshire. There are lots of activities to try. Children team up in groups of six and learn to be superheroes!

Activities include:

- riding quad bikes
- judo
- building a shelter
- swimming
- climbing and abseiling
- learning to read a map and crack a code
- finding out about fire safety
- designing a superhero logo and printing it on a T-shirt.

The last day is a team competition. Each team has to find the secret plans and save the world!

Tips!

Don't go on this holiday if:
- you are worried about staying away from home
- you like to do your own thing
- you like a quiet life.

Important information

Number of weeks	Accommodation	Weather conditions	Things you need
1	Shared dormitories	Warm Sunshine and showers	Old, comfortable clothing Trainers Waterproofs Your teddy!

Travel with a Twist

'Travel with a Twist' is a new holiday company that sells 'different' holidays. They have asked you to test one of the holidays. You can choose one of three holidays for four people.

Think before you choose!

There are lots of things to think about before you decide which holiday is best for you.

- The people you are taking with you – their tastes, interests and ages.
- The location – what sort of place is it? How long will it take to get there?
- The accommodation – will everyone be comfortable?
- The weather
- The activities – will you and your companions enjoy them?
- The cost – will you need expensive equipment?

Get close to the wildlife in the Kruger National Park

Stay in the amazing Icehotel and drive a husky sledge

Go diving with sharks

Conservation Volunteer

The National Parks of Africa help to protect endangered animals and plants. On this holiday, volunteers can help at the Kruger National Park, South Africa.

You will help the rangers and vets to:

- mend fences
- count game from an aeroplane
- go on an elephant safari
- camp and hike in the National Park
- tag birds of prey
- meet and work with local people and learn about their traditional way of life.

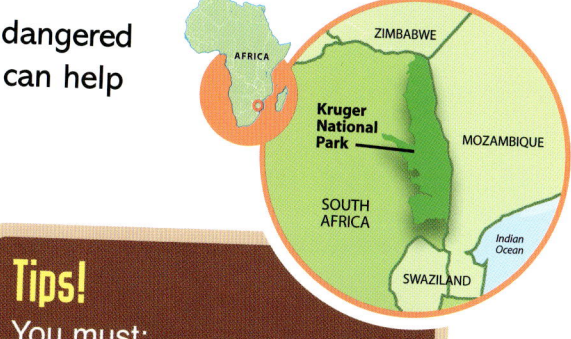

Tips!
You must:
- have a sense of adventure
- not be afraid of mucking in.

Important information

Number of weeks	Location	Accommodation	Weather conditions			Things you need
			Spring (Sep–Nov)	Summer (Dec–Feb)	Autumn (Mar–May)	
4	Kruger National Park, South Africa	Bungalow Tent (when camping)	Warm Sunny Light rain 23°C	Hot Sunny Light rain 27°C	Warm Sunny Light rain 23°C	Natural coloured clothes Walking boots Sunscreen Insect repellent Torch Light waterproofs Camera!

Drive a Husky Sledge!

You will spend your first night in Lapland at the Icehotel, and experience living in a building made entirely of ice. The next day, you can learn to drive a husky dog sledge, sledging through the snowy forest to observe wildlife. Then you will drive back in a snowmobile.

Tips!
Husky dogs are friendly but fast – you may fall out of your sledge!

Icehotel factfile
- The Icehotel is built each November and melts each spring.
- It is made from 3,000 tonnes of ice and 20,000 cubic metres of snow.
- The temperature inside is -5°C.

Optional activities
- reindeer-spotting trip
- building an igloo
- night-time excursion to view the Northern Lights (not guaranteed)

Important information

Number of days	Location	Accommodation	Weather conditions	Things you need
4	Lapland	Icehotel Wilderness lodge	Very cold: -35°C to -25°C (Winter only: Dec and Jan)	Full Arctic clothing provided

Dive with Sharks!

The highlight of this holiday in the Bahamas is the chance to dive with sharks. Many divers are surprised at how gentle these creatures seem – although sharks always deserve respect.

You can try cage-diving or experience the excitement of cage-free diving. You will see reef sharks, hammerhead sharks and tiger sharks, and can take photographs using underwater cameras.

Tips!
You must be a confident swimmer with scuba diving experience.

This holiday includes:
- observing sharks in the wild
- underwater shark-feeding trips
- a shipwreck dive.

Diving glossary
Cage-diving – viewing sharks from inside a cage.
Cage-free diving – swimming free with sharks.

Important information

Number of days	Location	Accommodation	Weather conditions	Things you need
7	The Bahamas	Ship's cabin	Very warm: 20°C to 32°C (all year) Tropical storms in summer	Diving equipment provided

Fizzy Stuff

How to Make Hokey Pokey

Hokey Pokey is a sweet from New Zealand. It's crunchy and crumbly. You can just eat it, or crumble it over ice cream. Don't forget to brush your teeth afterwards!

Equipment

- Foil
- A dish
- A tablespoon
- A teaspoon
- A large heavy saucepan
- A long-handled wooden spoon
- A timer
- Oven gloves

Ingredients

- 5 tablespoons of sugar
- 2 tablespoons of golden syrup
- 1 teaspoon of bicarbonate of soda

WARNING!

- Always ask a grown-up to help you make Hokey Pokey.
- Take care – the mixture gets **very hot**.
- Remember to wear oven gloves!

What to do

1. Put the foil on your dish.
2. Heat up the sugar and golden syrup in the saucepan. Keep stirring all the time.
3. When it starts to boil, turn the heat down very low. Cook it very gently for 4 minutes. Stir it from time to time. Don't let it boil.
4. Take it off the heat.
5. Stir in the bicarbonate of soda. It will fizz up. Pour it quickly into the dish.
6. When it is cold, break the Hokey Pokey into bits and eat it. Don't forget to save the crumbly bits for ice cream!

Bella's Volcano

Bella made something rather surprising at the weekend! Here's what she told her friend Jamie about it.

Bella Hey, Jamie! You'll never guess what I did at the weekend!

Jamie Go on then, tell me.

Bella I made a volcano!

Jamie A *volcano*? No way!

Bella Yes I did! I made it in the garden. First I made the earth really wet. Then I piled it up like a sandcastle. I made it into a cone shape so that it would look like a real volcano.

Jamie I bet you got really muddy!

Bella Yes – but Mum didn't mind. I made a hole in the top of the cone with my finger. Then I put two teaspoons of bicarbonate of soda inside the hole, and poured a big glug of vinegar on top. Guess what happened?

Jamie What?

Bella The vinegar made the bicarbonate of soda fizz up and pour down the sides. It looked just like a real volcano!

Jamie I wouldn't mind having a go at that, but there's just one problem – we don't have a garden.

Bella Never mind – perhaps we can think of somewhere else you could make it …

11

Tip of the Tongue

How to Make an Electric Lemon

Electricity from a lemon? Strange – but true! Here's how to do it.

Equipment
- 1 lemon
- paperclip
- thick piece of copper wire

What to do

1. Ask a grown-up to cut off any plastic coating from the ends of the copper wire.

2. Straighten out the paperclip.

3. Roll the lemon gently on the table, without breaking the skin. This will get the juices moving around inside.

4. Now stick one end of the paperclip into the lemon.

5. Stick one end of the copper wire into the lemon, close to the paperclip. Make sure that the wire and the paperclip do not touch inside the lemon!

6. Touch the other end of the copper wire and the other end of the paperclip to your tongue at the same time. You'll feel a slight tingle on your tongue, which is caused by electricity!

How does it work?

You have made the lemon into an electric battery.

A battery needs two different kinds of metal and an acid. The two kinds of metal come from the wire and the paperclip, and the lemon juice contains acid. When you touch the wires to your tongue, the water in your saliva conducts electricity and completes the circuit. That's why you feel the electricity tingling!

Warning! NEVER touch live electric wires.

Candy Crystals

Jake grew some beautiful crystals using a mixture of sugar and water. He describes to his sister how he did it.

Elaine What's in this jar, Jake?

Jake Hey! Be careful – those are my sugar candy crystals!

Elaine What are you doing with them?

Jake Just watching them, I guess! Mum helped me grow them.

Elaine What did you have to do?

Jake Well, we started last week. Mum and I put some sugar and water in a saucepan, and boiled it up. Then Mum poured the mixture into a jam jar. We used about twice as much sugar as water.

Elaine But what's the pencil for? And what's that button doing there?

Jake Oh – I forgot to say that first of all I tied a piece of cotton string around the middle of a pencil. I threaded the button on to the end of the string, and put the pencil on top of the jar so that the string was dangling into the jar. I made it the right length so that the button didn't quite touch the bottom of the jar.

Elaine It sounds too complicated!

Jake No, it was easy! Anyway, when Mum poured in the hot sugar mixture, the string dangled into it. When the jar had cooled down, I put it on the windowsill. I had to cover it with a piece of kitchen towel to stop dust getting in. I've been looking at it every day for a whole week. It's really fascinating to see how the crystals grow on the string. Look – they're really big now.

Elaine What are you going to do with the crystals now?

Jake What do you think? Eat them, of course!

Spice Up Your Story: Lively Verbs

A thesaurus can help you choose lively verbs to make your writing more exciting. Watch out, though – make sure you know exactly what words mean before you use them!

Try not to use the same word all the time. In stories people **say** a lot and **move** a lot. If you're not careful, you end up always using the verbs **said** and **went**.

Beth's story

In the second story opening I used different verbs instead of "said" and "went".

Look at Beth's story:

On Tuesday I went to the park. I saw my friend. She said, "Do you want to play on the climbing tree?" We went over to the tree and went up it. "Don't go too high," I said to Kirsty. "You will get stuck."

Now look at this:

On Tuesday I walked to the park. I saw my friend. She asked, "Do you want to play on the climbing tree?" We ran over to the tree and clambered up it. "Don't go too high," I shouted to Kirsty. "You will get stuck."

Thesaurus

Here are some word lists from a thesaurus. Can you find any other words that Beth could have used in her story opening?

brought carried bore delivered took

changed altered transformed tweaked

climbed ascended went up descended (climbed down)

found discovered uncovered came across stumbled upon learned

hid concealed covered

jumped bounded sprang leaped pounced

lost misplaced dropped

made created constructed produced

opened unlocked undid revealed

said called exclaimed asked whispered

saw looked spied noticed spotted glimpsed watched

shouted screamed screeched yelled

mumbled muttered

started began launched

stopped ended finished prevented

went ran came moved travelled slouched sped crawled

Verbs are sometimes called 'doing words' and 'being words'.
Verbs like **ran**, **jump**, and **look** are 'doing words'.
Verbs like **is**, **was**, **feels**, and **lives** are 'being words'.

Spice Up Your Story: Expressive Adjectives

A thesaurus can be useful for finding the best possible words to use in your writing. You can choose from lists of words with similar meanings. However, be careful – words listed together in a thesaurus do not always mean exactly the same thing!

Well-chosen adjectives can really improve a piece of writing. However, sometimes people use the same ones again and again. Adjectives like 'bad', 'good', 'nice', and 'big' are useful, but if you use them too often your reader will get bored.

It's not a good idea to use too many adjectives all at once. They're hard to read, and you can end up confusing your reader. It's often more effective to choose just one really good adjective.

I put in some interesting adjectives – but I think I used too many!

Sam's story

Here is the first draft of a story opening Sam wrote:

The man walked along the road. It was a winter night. He saw a figure coming towards him in the darkness.

Now look at this:

I like this version now. I took out some of the adjectives, and found some other good ones in the thesaurus.

The tired, exhausted man walked along the narrow, thin road. It was a dark, dim, shadowy winter night. He saw a scary, spooky figure coming towards him in the darkness.

This is Sam's final draft:

The exhausted man walked along the narrow road. It was a starless winter night. He saw a strange figure coming towards him in the darkness.

Thesaurus

Here are some adjective word lists from a thesaurus. Can you find any other words that Sam could have used in his story opening?

Remember the main rule of using a thesaurus – you need to know what a word means before you use it.

Adjectives are words that describe somebody or something – words like **big**, **green**, **adventurous** etc.

annoying irritating infuriating
bad nasty horrible rotten disgusting frightening annoying evil wicked
beautiful delightful lovely handsome stunning gorgeous pretty
big huge enormous large bulky fat
clean fresh pure spotless
dirty filthy muddy greasy
fast quick sudden speedy rapid hasty
good excellent lovely fine great kind pleasant
great wonderful amazing fantastic brilliant
happy joyful cheerful glad delighted
heavy weighty hefty bulky
lazy idle sluggish
light weightless airy pale faint
long stretched extended lengthy
near close neighbouring
new recent modern unused original up-to-date
noisy loud ear-splitting turbulent
old elderly antique faded stale out-of-date
quiet peaceful calm gentle
scary frightening terrifying creepy
short small little tiny brief
small little tiny trivial minor minute
untidy scruffy shabby messy disorganised

The Viking Sword

Viking sword found buried in churchyard

Marie Ericson and (inset) the Viking sword

BUILDING work at a local church stopped yesterday when workmen found a sword buried by the east door.

Historians say it is a Viking weapon. "It's a huge thing, and beautifully made," said Marie Ericson, from the town museum.

"It was obviously owned by a great warrior, and he must have been very tall to be able to handle it. Vikings were often buried with their weapons, but this sword was just buried by itself, so what happened to its owner is anybody's guess. My family have lived in this area for generations, and I have a Viking name. I like to think that one of my ancestors might have known the person who owned this sword. It certainly gave me a very strange feeling when I lifted it up."

Letter from the priest Anselm to a nearby monastery

Anselm to His Grace the Abbot at the Abbey of St Swithin's, this 14th day of June in the year of Our Lord 866.

Your Grace,

I must tell you today of a great miracle which has befallen us. We have all prayed for the Viking raids on our villages along this coast to stop, but the Vikings came again last week, like wolves to sheep.

I gathered the people into the church and we prayed to be saved. The Vikings came to the East door and I went out to meet them. They were great tall men and their swords were out. Truly I did not think I would live to see the morning. But the tallest of them was being supported by two others, and I could see he was close to death. Then one Viking stepped forward and said: "We will make a bargain with you, priest. We have heard that you heal the sick. Our leader is sick. His leg is broken and he has a fever that will not stop. Let your God heal our leader and we will not bother your villages again."

Your Grace, what could I say? Except to point out that God does not make bargains. I agreed to look after the sick man. The Vikings went without one drop of blood being spilled. Their leader swung between life and death for two days but is now well on the mend. He has promised that when the Vikings return for him there will be no more bloodshed.
Praise be to God.

Anselm

Letter from the Viking Harald Ericson to his wife at home

Harald Ericson to his wife Thorni at Ribe in Denmark this second month of summer

My wife,

I am sending this letter with a fishing fleet who will call on our home village. I want you and our son to leave with the fleet and come to the village in England where I am.

I was dying, yet I live — saved by a Christian priest. He cured me, and now I feel I have a debt to pay. This priest and his god are strange. You cannot make bargains with the god. And you cannot frighten the priest. He has no weapon and yet he showed no fear of us, his enemies.

I want to follow this man, and I want you and the boy to be here. I have been offered a place on the land. It is good land and we will live well.

Now I must tell you a secret. Last night I took my sword and I buried it by the east door of the church. It was my father's, and his father's before him, but when I look into that priest's eyes I know I will never use a sword again. I buried it with all honour. I look forward to seeing you both again.

Your husband,
Harald Ericson

The Tudor Ring

Boy's dog collars a Tudor ring

EIGHT-YEAR-OLD Tyrone Smith is celebrating this week after finding a Tudor ring in the back garden of his Dover home.

Tyrone's dog Sally uncovered the ring while digging in the garden.

"I was really cross with her at first," Tyrone said yesterday. "Sally was digging like mad in mum's new flower bed and she was so excited she kept coming back and jumping up. She got mud all over my jeans. But when I finally pulled her away, I found the ring."

Experts at the town's museum say that the ring, made of gold, amber and silver, may even have belonged to Queen Elizabeth I. "There are pictures of her wearing something just like this," said a spokeswoman. "But we need to investigate further, and there will probably need to be an inquest. Normally, treasure trove belongs to the owner of the place where it was found, but sometimes a museum buys the object for a national collection. This is certainly a very valuable find."

Which is great news for Tyrone, who plays in a local steel band. "If I sell the ring, I could buy some new equipment for the band – and still have enough money to go on holiday with my mum and dad."

LUCKY FIND: Tyrone with Sally.

To Mistress Eleanor, serving woman, Hatfield Palace

My dear Mother,

Last night, I must tell you, I sang for the Queen. Can you imagine it? One of her ladies had heard me whistling in the corridor. When she sent for me, I expected to receive a thrashing. So did Father. He said he did not know whether to thrash me himself, or hug me to keep my courage up. He told me that many people think we are foreign because we are black, and they say we should be sent away, but I say that is folly, because where would we go? Father will only say that I am eight and cannot know everything.

You must know, that when I went in to see her Majesty I was wearing my best doublet; the one you made, and I made a bow that could not be bettered by the Earl of Leicester. Her ladies giggled behind their hands, but the Queen asked me to sing. And when I did, she smiled and said I must sing again at the banquet she was giving for the Portuguese ambassador, and that Father and his friend Dick Marsh must play too.

So we did. We sang and sang and the Queen called for more and pledged our health and then she called me over and took off one of her rings and gave it to me, and said I must sing again right soon. Father is very happy.

Your loving son,
Ben

To Dick Marsh, musician, Whitehall

My dearest friend Dick,

I write this letter in haste as our ship is going soon. My son Ben is so unhappy, and I cannot explain to him properly what has happened. You were away when the Queen decided to send us from England. Many people have been telling her that there are too many blacks in the country. And so she agreed to send us and some others to Portugal in exchange for English prisoners being held there. We do not know what to expect. We cannot speak Portuguese. We have lived all our lives in England. Ben was born here, and I was brought when I was a baby. Ben is so upset. When we stopped to eat on our way to Dover, Ben ran into the woods and took off the ring that the Queen gave him and hurled it away. I was cross at such a naughty thing. That ring could have bought us many meals in Portugal. But I had not the heart to thrash him. He was in tears already. We have met Eleanor, who was staying in the country, and sail tonight for our new life. Wish us God's speed.

Your great friend,

Thomas

Magical Cards: People

These cards are full of fascinating facts about people from myths and legends. Some of these characters have awesome powers. Watch out for those with a five-star magical power rating!

Anancy

Type of creature: part man, part spider!

What he is like: Anancy is a trickster. He tricks his way out of trouble.

Magical power rating: ★

Good or bad? Mostly bad

Centaur

Type of creature: top half human, bottom half horse

What they are like: Most centaurs are shy creatures. They stay away from people.

Magical power rating: ★

Good or bad? Can be either

Furies

Type of creature: women with wings, and snakes instead of hair

What they are like: The Furies punish people who do wrong things. They can be cruel.

Magical power rating: ★★★★★

Good or bad? A bit of both

Grendel

Type of creature: half man, half monster!

What he is like: Because of a magic spell, Grendel could not be killed by a sword. The hero Beowulf had to use his hands to kill Grendel.

Magical power rating: ★★★

Good or bad? Bad

Harpy

Type of creature: woman's face, body of a vulture

What they are like: Harpies smell horrible. Their claws are made of metal!

Magical power rating: ★★★

Good or bad? Bad

Leprechaun

Type of creature: magical little old man

What they are like: Leprechauns wear green. They like to hide gold, and play tricks on people.

Magical power rating: ★★

Good or bad? Can be either

Mermaid

Type of creature: half human, half fish

What they are like: Mermaids live in the sea, and have tails like fish. There have been stories about mermaids for about 9,000 years!

Magical power rating: ★★

Good or bad? Can be either

Sphinx

Type of creature: head of a woman, body of a lion

What she is like: The Sphinx asks riddles and kills people who give the wrong answer.

Magical power rating: ★★★

Good or bad? Bad

Thor

Type of creature: god

What he is like: Thor is the Norse god of thunder. The thunder is made by the bashing of his huge hammer. He is very strong and can fight giants and demons.

Magical power rating: ★★★★★

Good or bad? Can be either

Weretiger

Type of creature: part human, part tiger

What they are like: Weretigers are dead people who have changed into tiger people. People believe it is dangerous to call their name.

Magical power rating: ★★★★★

Good or bad? Bad

Werewolf

Type of creature: part human, part wolf

What they are like: Werewolves are people who turn into wolves when there is a full moon. They can only be killed by a silver bullet.

Magical power rating: ★★★★

Good or bad? Bad

Magical Cards: Mythical Creatures

Mythical creatures appear in stories from all around the world. They often have magical powers which they can use for good or evil. Some are quite gentle – but others are terrifying!

Can you work out why the cards have been arranged in this order on the page? What other ways of grouping the cards can you think of?

Basilisk

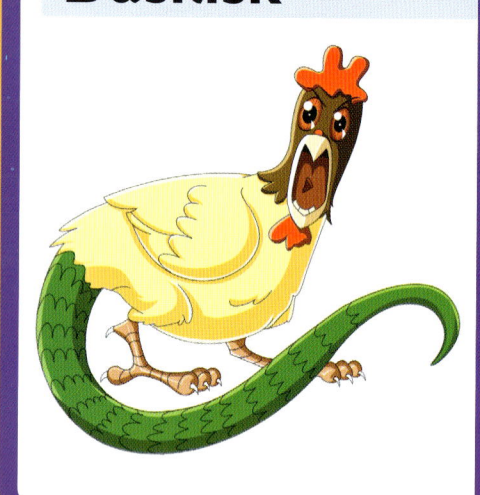

Type of creature: head, neck, wings and body of a hen, tail of a snake, with magical powers

Special features: The king of the serpents, part hen, part snake, sounds harmless, but it can kill anything in its path.

Magical power rating: 5

Good or bad? Bad

If you see a basilisk, hold your nose. Even its breath is deadly!

Boggart

Type of creature: magical creature similar to an elf or goblin

Special features: These tatty, hairy spirits live in people's houses, make mischief and cause accidents. There is no way to get rid of them, other than moving house.

Magical power rating: 3

Good or bad? Bad

Think twice before you invite a boggart to tea…

Cerberus

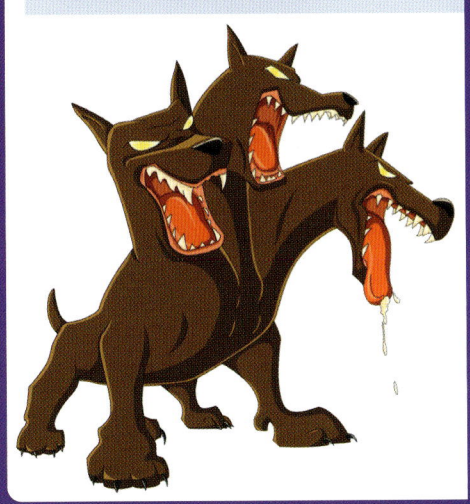

Type of creature: a terrifying three-headed dog

Special features: Cerberus guards the gates to the underworld. The Greek hero Orpheus tames him by playing sweet music on a lyre.

Magical power rating: 3

Good or bad? Bad

You'd better hope Cerberus shares your taste in music…

Chimera

Type of creature: the head of a lion, the body of a goat and the tail of a dragon

Special features: Some people believe this fire-breathing creature from Greek myth is the sister of the three-headed dog Cerberus.

Magical power rating: 3

Good or bad? Bad

Do you think Chimera sounds fierce? You should see her brother Cerberus!

Dragon

Type of creature: giant winged lizard

Special features: Dragons appear in lots of ancient legends. Dragons can breathe fire and often guard treasure.

Magical power rating: 4

Good or bad? Mostly bad

The rumble of fire-breath overhead… the flapping of giant leather wings… Take cover! It's a dragon!

Hippogriff

Type of creature: the front half of a bird, the back half of a horse, wings

Special features: Hippogriffs are the children of horses and griffins. They are sometimes used as a symbol of love.

Magical power rating: 2

Good or bad? Good

If you love someone… give them a hippogriff.

Hydra

Type of creature: fierce nine-headed water-dwelling monster

Special features: If you cut a head off, two more grow in its place. Heracles kills it by burning the stumps left after chopping the heads off, to stop more heads from growing.

Magical power rating: 4

Good or bad? Bad

The stench of the Hydra's breath alone would be enough to kill man or beast.

Jinn

Type of creature: magical shape-shifting creature

Special features: These creatures can take on the shape of any animal or person. They like playing tricks.

Magical power rating: 2

Good or bad? Can be either

Be careful if you meet a Jinn – there is no way of knowing what it will do next.

Phoenix

Type of creature: beautiful bird with red and gold wings

Special features: Every 500 years the phoenix burns itself to death and comes back to life as a baby bird, out of the ashes.

Magical power rating: 2

Good or bad? Good

As the old life ends, a new life is born from the ashes.

Selkie

Type of creature: seals that can take off their seal skin to reveal a beautiful human underneath

Special features: It is very bad luck to kill a selkie, but you can stop them getting away by stealing their seal skin.

Magical power rating: 1

Good or bad? Mostly good

The selkie longs to return to the sea.

Troll

Type of creature: giant man-eating beast

Special features: Trolls live under bridges and in caves. These horrible creatures come out at night to eat people passing over their bridge.

Magical power rating: 3

Good or bad? Bad

Walking home over a bridge in the dark? Be careful…

Index

abseiling	5	Queen Elizabeth I	21, 22
adjectives	16-17		
adventure park	5	recipes	10, 13
Alps	3	ring	21-23
Bahamas	9	sharks	9
bicarbonate of soda	10, 11	skiing	3
		snowboarding	3
Canada	4	South Africa	7
candy	13	sugar	10, 13
crystals	13	sweets	10, 13
		sword	18-20
diving	9		
		thesaurus	14-17
electricity	12	treasure trove	21
		Tudors	21-23
holidays	2-9		
husky dog	8	Vancouver Island	4
		verbs	14-15
Icehotel	8	Vikings	18-20
		volcano	11
judo	5		
		whales	4
Kruger National Park	7	Whitby	2, 5
Lapland	8		
lemon	12		
mythical creatures	28-31		
mythical people	24-27		